P9-CCJ-624

3117 5317

BIOGRAPHY
J
Sanford, William R.
Davy Crockett

Scott County Library System
Hdqrs: 215 N. 2nd Street
Eldridge, Iowa 52748

GAYLORD MG

BIOGRAPHY
J
CROCKETT

DAVY CROCKETT
DEFENDER OF
THE ALAMO

William R. Sanford &
Carl R. Green

ENSLOW PUBLISHERS, INC.

44 Fadem Road   P.O. Box 38
Box 699   Aldershot
Springfield, N.J. 07081   Hants GU12 6BP
U.S.A.   U.K.

Scott County Library System
Hdqrs: 215 N. 2nd Street
Eldridge, Iowa 52748

Copyright © 1996 by William R. Sanford and Carl R. Green

All rights reserved.

No part of this book may be reproduced by any means
without the written permission of the publisher.

Library of Congress Cataloging-in-Publication Data

Sanford, William R. (William Reynolds), 1927–
 Davy Crockett : defender of the Alamo / William R. Sanford and Carl R. Green.
  p. cm. — (Legendary heroes of the Wild West)
 Includes bibliographical references (p.)
 Summary: Relates the true story of Davy Crockett, one of the Old West's
outstanding hunters, frontiersmen, and legislators.
  ISBN 0-89490-648-8
  1. Crockett, Davy, 1786–1836—Juvenile literature. 2. Pioneers—
Tennessee—Biography—Juvenile literature. 3. Legislators—United
States—Biography—Juvenile literature. 4. United States. Congress.
House—Biography—Juvenile literature. 5. Alamo (San Antonio, Tex.) —
Siege, 1836. [1. Crockett, Davy, 1786–1836. 2. Pioneers. 3. Legislators.]
I. Green, Carl R. II. Title. III. Series: Sanford, William R. (William Reynolds), 1927–
Legendary heroes of the Wild West.
F436.C95S22 1996
976.8'04'092—dc20
[B]   95-36837
                                                              CIP
                                                               AC

Printed in the United States of America

10 9 8 7 6 5 4 3 2 1

Illustration Credits: Archives Division, Texas State Library, pp. 27, 31, 41;
Louise Dyer, The Crockett Tavern Museum, pp. 10, 13, 20; William R.
Sanford and Carl R. Green, pp. 6, 21, 24, 32, 36, 37, 40; Texas Department
of Transportation, p. 8; Western History Collection, University of Oklahoma,
pp. 12, 16, 29.

Cover Illustration: Paul Daly

Contents

8-96 Gutt If

3 0050 03117 5317

AUTHORS' NOTE

This book tells the true story of Davy Crockett. Davy was one of the Wild West's greatest heroes. In his day, he was known as an outstanding hunter, politician, storyteller, and soldier. His daring exploits were written up in the newspapers, magazines, and almanacs of the early 1800s. In more recent years, Davy has been featured in films, books, and a popular television series. You may be amazed to learn that one man could pack so much adventure into a single lifetime. If so, rest easy. All of the events described in this book really happened.

1

VICTORY OR DEATH!

~~~~~~~~~~~~~

Dawn came to San Antonio about six o'clock on March 6, 1836. Inside the Alamo, the old mission-turned-fortress, weary Texans checked their guns. The men had been under siege for twelve long, bloody days.

Davy Crockett stood on the south wall. A tall man in a coonskin cap, Davy was America's best-known frontiersman. He was there to help Texas win independence from Mexico. Freedom, Davy believed, was worth fighting for.

Eight hundred yards away, a red flag flew atop the San Fernando Church. Davy knew what the flag meant. General Antonio López de Santa Anna, Mexico's dictator, had vowed to take no prisoners. Victory lay within his grasp. The Texans were outnumbered, 2,400 to 183.[1]

Colonel William Travis commanded the Alamo. On February 24, he had called on Texans to come to his aid. Thirty-two fighting men from Gonzales had slipped into the Alamo on March 1. No further help had come. James Fannin had four hundred men under arms at Goliad, but he refused to risk the march to San Antonio.

Commander-in-chief Sam Houston had long ago given the Alamo up for lost. In January, he had ordered Colonel Travis to blow up the fortress. Travis had refused the order. He had prepared his men to fight to the finish. His only course, he said, was "Victory or death!"[2]

Santa Anna's troops advanced to the sound of bugles blowing the *deguello*. Like the red flag, the stirring music warned, "We take no prisoners."[3]

A hail of rifle and cannon fire poured down on the attackers. A Mexican soldier fell each time Davy's

Davy Crockett reached the Alamo in February 1836. He soon learned that Mexican troops were advancing on the fortress. Davy, who was America's most famous frontiersman, volunteered to stay and fight for Texas independence.

long-barreled rifle sang out. The enemy's muskets could not match Old Betsy's three hundred-yard range. The first wave slowed and fell back. Santa Anna rallied his men, and they returned to the attack. Texans were dying, too. Those who survived kept firing. They beat back the second assault.

Urged on by their officers, the assault troops carried their ladders forward a third time. Hundreds died, but many reached the walls. Waves of soldiers in blue-and-white uniforms poured into the fortress. With no time to reload, Texans swung their rifles like clubs. The Mexicans pressed forward behind blood-stained bayonets.

Davy and a handful of Texans made a last stand in the barracks. They fought behind a wall of mattresses, chairs, and tables. One by one, the defenders fell, dead or wounded. Mexican reports of the battle told what happened next. Their shot bags empty, Davy and a few survivors laid down their arms. General Manuel Castrillon stepped forward. He pledged that the prisoners would not be harmed.

The sight of the prisoners sent Santa Anna into a rage. He tongue-lashed Castrillon for breaking the "no prisoners" order. One of the Texans, Lieutenant Enrique de la Peña observed, was David Crockett. "Santa Anna," de la Peña wrote, "ordered [Crockett's] execution. . . . Several officers . . . thrust themselves forward, . . . and with swords in hand, fell upon these . . . defenseless men just as a tiger leaps upon his prey."[4]

The dictator's triumph cost him dearly. Six weeks later, Sam Houston's troops engaged the Mexicans at San

Jacinto. His troops screamed, "Remember the Alamo!" as they routed Santa Anna's forces. Texas had won its war for independence.

Americans did not want to hear that Davy had died a prisoner. By the end of the month, a story that denied the Mexican report was making the rounds. "David Crockett," a writer claimed, "was found dead with about twenty of the enemy with him and his rifle was broken to pieces."[5]

In the long run, the details do not matter. What counts is that this great American hero died fighting for freedom. Those who knew him were not surprised. From childhood on, Davy Crockett had been one of a kind.

Once the walls were breached, thousands of Mexican troops swept into the Alamo. Davy and a handful of defenders made their last stand in the barracks (right). He surrendered after his ammunition ran out. True to his boast, Santa Anna refused to take prisoners. He ordered his men to execute Davy and the other survivors.

2
A FRONTIER CHILDHOOD

The Crocketts came to America from Ireland in the 1700s. Around 1776 David Crockett moved from North Carolina to the northeast corner of Tennessee. His son John fought in the Revolutionary War. After the war, John and his wife Rebecca started their own farm on Limestone Creek. Along with corn and hogs, the Crocketts raised a fine crop of children. On August 17, 1786, their fifth son arrived. Rebecca and John named him David, after his grandfather.

John worked hard, but he never had much luck. In 1794 he built a small mill on Cove Creek. A flood washed the mill away that same year. John did not quit. He made a fresh start by opening a tavern on the Virginia-Knoxville road. Each night young Davy listened as travelers spun tall tales before bedding down. Soon the boy was telling stories of his own.[1] The habit stayed with Davy for the rest of his life.

By 1798 John and Rebecca had six sons and three daughters. Money was scarce. Davy helped feed the family with the game he bagged in the woods. When the boy was twelve, John hired him out to work for Jacob Siler. Siler paid Davy $5 for tending his cattle during the long journey to his farm in Virginia. When they arrived, Siler pressured Davy to stay with him. Unsure of his rights, the homesick boy agreed. Five weeks later, a friendly teamster helped Davy escape.

In 1799 John sent thirteen-year-old Davy to school. Before the week was out, Davy fought with the class bully.

Young Davy Crockett lived in this Morristown tavern after his father opened its doors in 1796. In the evening, chores finished, Davy sat spellbound as travelers told stories about life on the frontier. The boy soon acquired a lifelong habit of telling his own tales.

The punishment for fighting, he knew, was a whipping. Davy put off the beating by hiding in the woods each day. A week later the teacher sent a note home, asking about Davy. John picked up a hickory stick and ordered his son back to school. Davy took off running. He outran his father—and kept on going.

Davy made his way back to Virginia. Doing farm work paid twenty-five cents a day. After he had saved $7, he headed for Baltimore. There Davy saw the sea for the first time. That same day a sailing ship captain hired him as a cabin boy. Davy then went looking for teamster Adam Myers, who was holding his money. Myers put him off, saying he had spent the $7. Moved by Davy's tears, another teamster came to the boy's aid. Faced with a beating, Myers said he would repay the $7—when they reached Tennessee. Davy guessed that day would be a long time coming. Broke and discouraged, he gave up his dream of going to sea.[2]

For a time, Davy worked for a hatter. Eighteen months later, the man went broke. After that, odd jobs kept Davy fed and clothed. Nearly three years after leaving home, he walked into Crockett's Tavern. Hours passed before his sister Betsy recognized him. She gave him a big hug. His parents added their own warm welcome.

Davy went to work to pay John's debts. Six months of plowing fields and chopping wood paid off a $36 debt. A second six months retired a $40 debt. His duty done, Davy stayed with the second farmer as a hired hand. John Kennedy was a kind man—and he had a pretty niece. The girl made Davy's heart "flutter like a duck in a puddle."

Dressed in the fringed buckskins of the backwoodsman, Davy stands ready to venture into the Tennessee wilderness. Like many young men of his day, he was more at home in the wilderness than he was in town. In this painting, Davy is holding his long-barreled hunting rifle and a coonskin cap.

He set out to court her, only to learn that she was engaged. Instead of pining away, Davy went back to school. If he was better educated, he reasoned, girls would like him better. After six months, he said he could "read a little" and "cypher [do arithmetic] some."[3]

Davy was now a lean five feet, ten inches tall, brown-haired and blue-eyed. Girls liked his good looks and his sense of humor. In 1805 he took out a license to marry Margaret Elder. At the last minute, the bride-to-be jilted him. Davy was certain he would never find another girl to love.

Nine months later Polly Finley helped mend his heart. Davy met the pretty, red-haired girl at a country dance. A whirlwind courtship led to a wedding in 1806. The young couple set up housekeeping on a rented farm. Polly's dowry of two cows and two calves helped stock the farm.

Davy furnished the tiny cabin with a $15 credit at the general store.[4]

Davy and Polly soon started a family. John Wesley arrived in 1807. William followed in 1809. In 1811 Davy bought a five-acre farm in south-central Tennessee. Margaret was born there the next year. In 1813 the Crocketts moved again. This time a flatboat carried them to the Elk River country. Beyond Tennessee's southern border, trouble was brewing.

Davy paid for a marriage license in 1805, but the girl jilted him. A year later, he took out this license to marry Polly Finley. The young couple set up housekeeping on a rented farm. Polly gave birth to their first child there a year later.

3

CAMPAIGNING WITH GENERAL JACKSON

~~~~~~~~~~~~~~~~~~~~~

Davy was one of thousands of settlers who lived west of the Appalachians. The push into the wilderness led to frequent clashes with Native Americans. Most of the settlers wanted the tribes to pack up and move west.

Two Native American brothers dug in their heels. Tecumseh and Prophet urged the tribes to drive out the settlers. The fiery Tecumseh said, "They seize your land. They corrupt your women. . . . Back whence they came, upon a trail of blood, they must be driven."[1]

In Alabama, Tecumseh's words stirred up the Creek. Bands of warriors painted their war clubs scarlet and went on the warpath. Frightened settlers called them Red Sticks. In August 1813, a Red Stick raid surprised the guards at Fort Mims. Over five hundred men, women, and children died that day.

News of the massacre alarmed Davy. He said he was going to join the local militia. Polly urged him not to leave her alone with three youngsters. Davy told her he could not let the Red Sticks scalp women and children.[2] In late September, he signed on for ninety days with the Tennessee mounted militia.

Davy was picked to serve as a scout. He was out in the woods one day when he met a friendly Creek. The man said he had seen a Red Stick war party. Davy rode at a breakneck pace to bring the news to Colonel John Coffee. To Davy's disgust, Coffee refused to act. Then Major John Gibson rode in with the same news. Convinced at last, Coffee sent a report to General Andrew Jackson. Jackson's men searched in vain for the Red Sticks. The local Creek, it turned out, had made up the story. They hoped the futile chase would keep the militia soldiers far from their villages.[3]

Coffee's men took bloody revenge for Fort Mims that November. After a brief skirmish, the soldiers closed in on a Red Stick camp. Outgunned and outnumbered, the warriors offered to give up. As the soldiers approached, a woman killed a young officer with an arrow. The soldiers instantly riddled her with bullets. Then they set fire to her lodge. Forty-six Red Sticks had been hiding inside. They all burned to death.[4]

Davy went home on leave. After a brief visit with Polly, he returned to finish his enlistment. When he was released on Christmas Eve, the army paid him $65.59.[5]

Andrew Jackson, war hero and future president, won national popularity during the War of 1812. Davy served a six-month enlistment during the war, but gained little glory. It was his lively sense of humor that distinguished him. Jackson praised Davy for keeping "the camp alive with his wit."

~~~~~~~~~~~~~~~~

To Davy, that was a small fortune. "I had done Indian fighting enough for one time," he said.[6]

In September 1814, Davy again ignored Polly's pleas. This time he signed up for a six-month tour of duty. "I wanted a small taste of British fighting," he said.[7]

The United States had been at war with Great Britain since 1812. Third Sergeant Crockett was sent to Florida with the Tennessee Mounted Gunmen. At the time, Florida belonged to Spain. Even so, the English were using Pensacola as a naval base.

The Gunmen joined a force that easily captured the port. The soldiers arrived the day after the British withdrew. Davy wrote that the whiskey flowed freely that night. The rest of the campaign was tougher. Davy and his friends chased small bands of Seminole through the swamps. When supplies ran short, Davy turned hunter.

His deadeye shooting brought down deer and wild tur-keys. Friendly Seminole traded corn for powder and shot.

In February 1815, Davy heard that Polly was sick. He returned home to find her burning with fever. He thought his heart would break when she died a few weeks later. The army called Davy back to duty, but he would not leave his children. He paid a young man to take his place. No one thought less of him, as the practice was legal at the time.[8]

Later, when he ran for office, Davy described his army career in heroic terms. In truth, he played only a minor role in the War of 1812. He earned true military fame years later at the Alamo.

4

A FRESH START

~~~~~~~~~~~~~~~~~~~~

At twenty-nine, Davy had filled out. He now carried one hundred ninety pounds on his tall, sturdy frame. His nose was sharp, and he had a pointed chin. He was proud of his ruddy cheeks, a sign of robust good health. Few could resist his lively sense of humor. During the Creek War, Andrew Jackson said, Davy "kept the camp alive with his wit."[1]

Davy needed a wife and his children needed a mother. A handsome young widow soon caught his eye. Elizabeth Patton had lost her husband in the Creek War. His death left her with a two hundred-acre farm, two young children, and $800 in cash. Davy and Elizabeth wed in the summer of 1815. The groom was now a man of substance. The owner of a two hundred-acre farm could serve in the state legislature.[2]

Davy had little reason to regret his choice. Elizabeth managed their affairs with thrift and common sense. Over the next six years, she also gave birth to three daughters and a son. Thanks in part to Elizabeth's modest fortune, Davy's neighbors gave him increased respect. In 1815 the men of Franklin County elected him a lieutenant of the militia.

Before long Davy became convinced that the region's climate was unhealthy. He and some friends rode south to look for a better place to live. While camping one night, the party's horses wandered off. Davy tracked the horses through creeks and bogs, but could not catch them. Worn out, he collapsed beside the trail. The chills and fever of malaria wracked his body. Luckily, some Creek hunters found him. Davy paid them to take him to a settler's cabin. With no doctor nearby, the settler's wife dosed him with a strong patent medicine. It was the woman's tender care, however, that pulled Davy through. The fever broke at last.

While Davy mended, one of his friends made his way home. The man did not know what had happened to Davy. He told Elizabeth that her husband was dead and buried. Weeks later she thought she was seeing a ghost when Davy walked in the door. Davy did not blame her. "I was so pale, . . . my face looked like it had been half-soled with brown paper," he wrote.[3]

Davy gave up on Alabama. Early in 1817, he leased his two farms and moved eighty miles west. Before long a number of Crocketts and Pattons joined him at Shoal

At Shoal Creek, everyone pitched in to construct sturdy log cabins. Davy and Elizabeth also built a small business empire. Neighbors brought their corn to the Crockett's gristmill to have it ground into meal. Surplus cornmeal ended up at Davy's whiskey distillery. The Crocketts also ran a gunpowder factory at Shoal Creek.

Creek. Davy's parents sold their tavern and moved there, too.

Davy and Elizabeth carved out a small business empire at Shoal Creek. After they cleared their land, they built a water-powered gristmill. Their neighbors paid them to grind their corn. Each day Elizabeth turned about fourteen bushels of corn into cornmeal. Much of the cornmeal went to Davy's distillery. His workers mixed the cornmeal with water and allowed it to ferment. A wood-fired still then turned the mash into whiskey.

A gunpowder factory was Davy's next project. Before long his crew was turning out seven thousand five hundred pounds of gunpowder a year. Davy sold the powder for thirty seven cents a pound. A hunter could get off ninety-six shots with a pound of Davy's powder.[4]

In the fall of 1818, Davy added public service to his workload. His first office was that of justice of the peace. As a justice of the peace, he performed marriages and sentenced thieves to be whipped. He also compiled the tax rolls. Later Davy claimed that his judgments were always fair. No one, he bragged, ever appealed them.[5]

Next came a greater honor. The men of the 57th Regiment of Militia elected Davy as their commandant. He took great pleasure in being called Colonel Crockett. He also found a new passion—running for office.

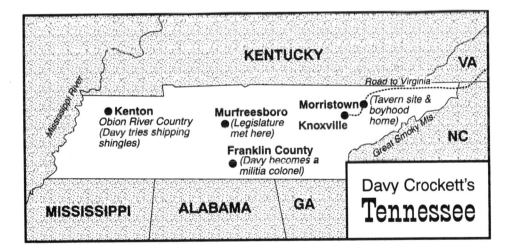

Davy Crockett left marks of his passage all across Tennessee. Whenever he had a business setback, he moved west to open a new frontier. At each stop along the way, he added to his reputation for honesty, straight shooting, and storytelling.

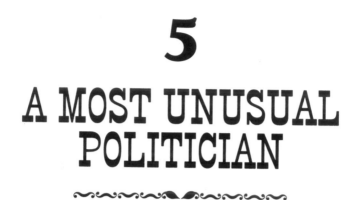

5

A MOST UNUSUAL POLITICIAN

In June of 1821, Davy launched a campaign for the state legislature. The backwoods politician did not pretend to know much about state politics. He filled his short speeches with funny stories. Standing on a stump and speaking to a crowd was a scary feeling. At times, Davy said, "I choked up as bad as if my mouth had been . . . cramm'd chock full of dry mush."[1]

After he spoke, Davy often asked the crowd to join him for a drink. Wealthy landowners laughed at him. The poor farmers of his district laughed—and drank—with him. Davy was elected by a margin of 2 to 1.

The Tennessee legislature met at Murfreesboro in September. Davy quickly spoke up for the rights of poor farmers. Many were in danger of losing their farms. The problem had started when North Carolina issued warrants during the Revolution. At that time Tennessee was part of

North Carolina. These warrants gave veterans the right to claim federal lands in Tennessee. If a warrant-holder filed for a piece of land, the farmer who was working it had to leave. Davy managed to slow this practice, but could not stop it.

Back home, a fall flood swept away his mill and gunpowder plant. Davy rode home to inspect the damage. "[The mills] had cost me upwards of three thousand dollars," he wrote. "[This was] more than I was worth in the world." Davy and Elizabeth sold some of their land to pay their debts. They also had to give up their cabin. Elizabeth did not despair. "Just pay up as long as you have a bit's worth in the world," she told Davy. "Then . . . we will scuffle for more."[2]

When the legislative session ended, Davy went looking for a new home. With his son John Wesley at his side, he headed west. He found what he wanted near the Obion River in the northwest corner of Tennessee. Eleven years earlier, an earthquake had toppled thousands of trees. Game thrived in the tangled undergrowth. Father and son staked their claim in the spring of 1822. Then they cleared a field and planted a corn crop. The nearest neighbor was seven miles away.

In May some supporters gave Davy a fine new rifle. This was the gun that later came to be called Old Betsy. In July he returned to the capital. He again fought the hated land warrants and backed aid to widows and children. When a bill to outlaw gambling came to a vote, Davy

After a flood destroyed his Shoal Creek buildings, Davy and his son John Wesley headed west. They staked a claim, built a cabin, and planted a crop in Tennessee's northwest corner. Davy's deadeye shooting kept father and son well provided with meat, hides, and furs.

opposed it. He saw no harm in betting on cards, horses, or a shooting match.[3]

By September Davy was home again. To feed the family and to raise cash, he hunted bear, deer, and wolves. He killed one black bear, he swore, that weighed six hundred pounds. Each wolf he killed brought in a $3 bounty. Davy sold the deerhides and bearskins. He used the money to buy coffee, sugar, salt, and gunpowder.

Davy did not want a second term. He was amazed, therefore, when a newspaper said he was planning to run. The story was meant as a joke, but Davy took it to heart. He told Elizabeth he would go hunting for votes instead of skins.

During the campaign, Davy heard his opponent give the same speech day after day. One day, Davy asked to speak first. Then he stood up and gave his opponent's speech, word-for-word. The trick, Davy said, left the man "speechless."[4]

Davy also liked to describe the hunting shirt he used to woo voters. One huge pocket held "a peck of tobacco." The other, he said, held a bottle of whiskey.[5] The non-existent shirt became part of Davy's growing legend.

The voters gave Davy an easy victory. Back in Murfreesboro, he fought for his backwoods farmers. He voted to reduce taxes and to improve waterways. Although Davy worked hard at his job, he was often bored. If a debate droned on too long, he wandered off to find a tavern or a card game.[6]

Davy's second term ended in October 1824. By then he had his sights set on a better job. He was thinking about running for Congress.

6

A BEAR HUNTER RUNS FOR CONGRESS

~~~~~~~~~~~~~~~~~~~~~~

Davy was not sure he should run for Congress. On his doubtful days, he moaned, "I knowed nothing about Congress matters."[1]

The presidential election of 1824 helped him make up his mind. In a four-way race, Andrew Jackson fell short of a majority in the electoral college. With no clear winner, the House of Representatives had to step in. When the House voted, Henry Clay used his influence to elect John Quincy Adams as president.

Tennessee had voted for Jackson, who was a hero there. As outrage swept the state, Davy saw his chance. Adam Alexander was the man he had to beat in 1825. The wealthy planter had voted for Clay's high tariffs. To farmers, high tariffs meant higher prices for imported goods.

The voters, candidate Crockett found, had to be courted. Alexander could afford to buy drinks after a rally. Davy campaigned with empty pockets. Legend says that he once traded a raccoon skin for a quart of whiskey. When the crowd asked for more, Davy stole the skin and sold it again. Later he bragged that he swiped and resold the same skin ten times.[2]

Davy lost the election by 267 votes. It was his bad luck that times were good. Cotton sold for twenty-five cents a pound that year. Alexander took the credit. He told farmers they could thank high tariffs for their fine year. Davy had to admit that his opponent knew a trick or two.

An old song says that Davy "killed him a bear when he was only three." That is a tall tale, of course. What is true is that Davy grew up to be a master hunter. After the election, he took his dogs into the woods. Old Whirlwind,

A children's song tells us that Davy "killed him a bear when he was only three." That's a tall tale, of course—but it does contain a germ of truth. As this old engraving reminds us, Colonel Crockett was recognized as a master tracker and marksman. There is no reason to doubt his claim that he once killed 105 bears in a single winter.

Grim, and Deathmaul treed many a bear for him.[3] By the end of winter Davy claimed to have killed 105 bears.

Once, on a cold, wet day, he stopped to build a tiny fire. The flames scarcely warmed his hands. How could he keep from freezing? As Davy tells the story, he found a tree with a smooth trunk and climbed it. Then he locked his arms around the trunk and slid down. Rubbing against the tree "made the insides of my legs and arms feel mighty warm and good," he claimed.[4]

The hunting was good, but the price of furs was falling. Davy turned to selling the narrow strips of wood, called staves, used to make barrels. He made plans to float some thirty thousand of these staves to New Orleans on two flatboats. Buyers there were paying good prices for staves and lumber. In January of 1826, Davy and his crew sailed smoothly down the Obion. It was on the mighty Mississippi that Davy made a fatal error. The flatboats became hard to steer after he ordered his men to lash them together. At Devil's Elbow, the boats hit a snag and broke apart. Davy was trapped in the cabin and almost drowned. His cargo of staves floated on down the river.

The shipwreck cost Davy at least $100. It did not cost him his sense of humor. He said that when he got to Congress he would pass a new law. His bill would "prevent fools from going into the wood stave business."[5]

With an eye on the voters, Davy worked to improve his image. When hands were needed to build a road, Davy volunteered. When men were needed for jury duty, the judge knew he could count on Davy. Elizabeth could have used him at home. She had to hire a man to help with the farmwork.

In 1827 Davy made a second run for Congress. Once again Adam Alexander was the man to beat. William Arnold and John Cook made it a four-way race. Cook accused Davy of being a drunk and a gambler. Davy hit back. He told even bigger lies about Cook. To clear his name, Cook brought a witness to one of Davy's rallies. Davy was not rattled. He agreed that he had lied—but only because Cook had started it. Both of us, he told a cheering crowd, are liars.[6]

The other candidates ignored Davy. No one, they sneered, would vote for a crude backwoodsman. In August Davy proved them wrong. He beat Alexander by more than two thousand votes. Colonel Davy Crockett was on his way to Congress!

~⌇⌇⌇⌇⌇◆⌇⌇⌇⌇⌇~

Davy started his political career by serving as a state legislator. In 1825, he raised his sights and ran for Congress. He lost that election by 267 votes. Two years later, he ran again. All but his close friends and neighbors were surprised when the "crude backwoodsman" outpolled his opponents.

7

"I CAN WALK LIKE AN OX, RUN LIKE A FOX"

Davy's career in Congress nearly ended before it began. In October 1827, during his trip to Washington, he fell ill with a fever. A doctor treated the fever by bleeding the patient. The loss of blood kept Davy in bed for a month. When he did reach the capital, the fever returned. Congress was in session when he finally took his seat.

There was nothing modest about Davy. In a speech to the House of Representatives he said, "I say, Mr. Speaker: I can outspeak any man on this floor and give him two hours start. I can outlook a panther, outstare a flash o'lightnin', tote a steamboat on my back, and play at rough and tumble with a lion. I can walk like an ox, run like a fox, spout like a volcano, and swallow a man whole if you butter his head and pin his ears back."[1]

Davy paid $1 a day for room and board at Mrs. Ball's Boarding House. If he drank Mrs. Ball's whiskey, the price doubled to $2. Although he dressed in city clothes, Davy's manners marked him as a backwoodsman. Did he drink from his finger bowl at a state dinner? Davy denied the story.[2] The public thought it was true—and loved him for it.

The slow pace in Congress made Davy restless. He sometimes drank and gambled when he should have been working. The record shows that he missed fifty-eight roll call votes in his first term. His pay of $8 a day did not cover his expenses. By the end of the session, Davy was $700 in debt.

Thomas Chilton was a fellow boarder at Mrs. Ball's. The congressman from Kentucky admired Davy. When his friend was mocked as a country bumpkin, Chilton turned ghostwriter. With his help, Davy's speeches became more polished. Chilton later served as his editor when Davy wrote his life story.

In Congress Davy

Davy preferred buckskins, but he put on city clothes when he went to Washington, D.C. As a congressman, he pushed for a bill to aid poor farmers. Special interests defeated the bill. That defeat, plus the slow pace at which Congress moved, left Davy feeling restless. He missed fifty-eight roll call votes in his first term.

Davy thought his fellow congressmen were inclined to put on airs. He argued that the country would be better off if it listened to him. The public read his colorful speeches and agreed. The speech in which he said he could "outstare a flash o' lightnin', tote a steamboat on my back, and play rough and tumble with a lion" was widely quoted.

worked hard to pass the Tennessee Vacant Land Bill. The bill was as straightforward as Davy himself. If it passed, Tennessee would take title to all vacant federal lands in the state. The next step would be to sell the land to poor farmers. The money raised would go to the schools. As he studied the bill, Davy saw a problem. What if the state set the price too high? He asked James Polk and his committee to write safeguards into the bill. Polk refused. Land speculators were shaping the bill to their own needs.

In April 1828, Davy spoke in support of the bill. "The rich require but little legislation," he scolded. "We should, at least occasionally, legislate for the poor."[3] The other side argued that giving away federal land would set a bad precedent. In the end, the bill never came to a vote.

Davy did not give up. He went back to Polk's committee. The government should give one hundred sixty acres to each settler in Tennessee's Western District, he said. The plan fell on deaf ears. The House adjourned in May without acting on the free land proposal.

During the summer, Davy moved his family to a new farm. He also began work on a new gristmill. This time he took the danger of flooding into account. Davy built his new mill well back from the river. Teams of horses turned the heavy grindstones.

In January 1829, Davy was back at work. He tried to add his free land amendment to the Public Lands Bill. His opponents worked just as hard to kill the plan. Some saw a threat to states' rights. Others worried that reduced land sales would take funding from the schools. After nine days of bitter debate, the House again set the bill aside.

Davy stayed in Washington to see Andrew Jackson sworn in as president. By late March, he was home again. Elizabeth was pleased to see that he had cut back on his drinking. His neighbors cheered him for sponsoring the Vacant Land Bill. Davy felt good about his chances for reelection.

8

WINS AND LOSSES

~~~~~~~~~~~~~~~~~~~~~~~~~~~

In August of 1829, the voters gave Davy a second term. His victory did not please the Jackson camp. The president's friends saw Davy as a threat to their control of the state. If the land bill became law, Davy would be a bigger hero than ever.[1]

Davy had rejoiced when Jackson won the White House. Now his ties to the president were weakening. Jackson's men went all out to defeat his land bill. Davy wrote that he still loved the president, despite the conflict. Then he added, "[I cannot] be compelled to love everyone who . . . pretends to rally around the Jackson standard."[2]

With the bill going nowhere, Davy tried a new tactic. In December 1829, he arranged to have the bill moved to a special committee—with himself as chairman. The committee voted to allow settlers in Tennessee's Western District to purchase up to two hundred acres. The price was set at twelve and a half cents an acre. The new bill failed, too. It finally passed in 1841—long after Davy's death. His son John Wesley, who followed him to Congress, pushed it through.[3]

By 1830 Davy's break with Jackson was complete. More than ever he spoke out for the rights of the poor. In one battle, he took aim at West Point. Only the sons of the wealthy, he charged, went to the military academy. These "gentlemen," he said, were "too nice for hard service."[4]

Congress ignored his half truths. West Point stayed open. Davy also lost his fight to give pensions to Revolutionary War militiamen. The aging volunteers should receive the same treatment as army vets, he argued. The House buried the bill, 122 to 56.

In May Davy stood up to defend the rights of Native Americans. President Jackson wanted to force five southeastern tribes to move west. The plan was meant to clear the way for land-hungry farmers. Davy argued that the United States should honor treaties made with the tribes. He said, "If I should be the only member of that House who voted against the bill, . . . I would still vote against it."[5] The bill passed despite his protests.

The failure of the land bill, plus his break with Jackson, hurt Davy. His easy win in 1829 turned into an uphill struggle in 1831. Lawyer William Fitzgerald, a Jackson man, ran an ugly campaign. Fitzgerald charged that Davy was a drunk, a fraud, and a gambler. He said Davy had cheated taxpayers by missing too many votes in the

House. Davy vowed to punch "Little Fitz" if he told more lies.

At a rally in the town of Paris, Tennessee, Fitzgerald spoke first. When he repeated his charges, Davy jumped up and started toward him. The lawyer drew a pistol. He threatened to shoot Davy if he came closer. Unsure for once of what to do, Davy went back to his seat. The news of the face-off spread like wildfire. Davy, the story went,

Davy lost his seat in Congress in 1831. Two years later, a poor cotton crop left steamboats with little cotton to pick up. Voters rallied behind Davy and sent him back to Congress. He tried once again to pass his land bill—and once again, it was defeated.

Leaders of the Whig party (shown here) studied Davy's popularity and talked about running him for president. In the end, the party turned to another candidate.

had looked old and tired.[6] In August he lost a close race by 595 votes.

At forty-five, Davy did not feel old. Over the next two years, he mended his political fences. By 1833 the voters were on his side again. A poor cotton crop had left farmers deeply in debt. Money was scarce, and banks had little cash to loan. In a close race, Davy regained his seat in Congress by 173 votes.

Davy pushed again for his land bill, but his old fire was missing. More than ever, he worked on his public image. In his speeches, he posed as the simple backwoodsman who stood up to President Jackson. "Look at my neck," he wrote. "You will not find there any collar, with the engraving 'MY DOG. Andrew Jackson.' "[7]

Back home, Davy's friends were worried. They warned that Jackson's Democratic party might deny him a fourth term. Davy was riding too high to listen. Leaders in the Whig party were wining and dining him. There was talk of running "the honest woodsman" for president.[8]

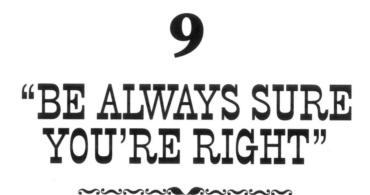

9

"BE ALWAYS SURE YOU'RE RIGHT"

Americans loved Davy's tall tales—and half-believed them. If Davy said he could "grin" a raccoon out of a tree, few would doubt him. In 1834, with Thomas Chilton's help, Davy wrote his life story. The book retold Davy's adventures and blasted his foes. *Narrative of the Life of Davy Crockett of the State of Tennessee, Written by Himself*, became a best-seller.

In the spring of 1834, Davy toured the major cities of the East. At Bunker Hill, he said he felt he was standing on holy ground.[1] In Philadelphia his fans gave him a fine new rifle. Davy named the gun Pretty Betsy. He described the trip in *An Account of Col. Crockett's Tour to the North and Down East*. That book, too, was a best-seller.

The almanacs of the day printed weather and crop information. As Davy's fame grew, the almanacs increased sales by adding tall tales of his exploits. Did Davy cross the Mississippi on stilts? Did he fight the Battle of New Orleans from the back of an alligator? The Crockett almanacs swore he did.

Wooden-legged Adam Huntsman challenged Davy in the election of 1835. "Timber Toes" raked up all the old tales of Davy's drinking and gambling. Davy mostly ignored the charges. He toured the district, telling stories and basking in the warmth of the crowds. To his surprise, the old tactics did not work. Davy lost his seat by 252 votes. The Jackson camp, he protested, had paid $25 a head for Huntsman's winning votes.[2]

During the campaign, Davy had made a promise. If elected, he said he would give the voters his best. If not, the voters "might all go to hell, and I would go to Texas."[3] Davy was drawn by the lure of cheap land. Here was a chance to pay off debts and make a new start.

Davy was as good as his word. He grabbed Old Betsy and set out for Texas. By the time he reached the Texas border, he was low on cash. He solved the problem by swapping his watch for a cheaper one and $30. By then his party had grown to sixteen or more "Crockett men." All had heard the same rumors. Texas would soon fight for its freedom from Mexico.

At each stop, Davy was hailed as a hero. In Nacogdoches, he and his friends took an oath of loyalty to Texas. On February 6, 1836, the party reached San Antonio. At the Alamo, the garrison threw a *fandango* in Davy's honor. The dance was in full swing when a messenger rode in with a warning. The Mexican army was advancing toward San Antonio.

General Santa Anna laid siege to the Alamo on February 23. The Texans held his forces at bay for thirteen long, bloody days. Davy was everywhere, urging the men to do their duty. The final assault breached the walls on March 6. The defenders died to the last man.

Davy Crockett died a hero's death that day in 1836. Since then, his story has been told and retold in books,

Davy replayed his old role of backwoods hero in the election of 1835. If he lost, he told voters, he would leave Tennessee and go to Texas. He did lose—and he kept his word. After the election, he grabbed his rifle, gathered a few friends, and headed for Texas. Ahead lay San Antonio and the Alamo.

The nation took Davy to its heart after he died. Readers snapped up "almanacks" like this 1837 edition that featured pictures and stories of the fallen hero. Today, a century and a half after his death, Davy lives on in books, television, and films.

Vol. I. "Go Ahead!" No. 3.
Davy Crockett's 18 ALMANACK, 37
OF WILD SPORTS IN THE WEST,
Life in the Backwoods, & Sketches of Texas.

O KENTUCKY! THE HUNTERS OF KENTUCKY!!!
Nashville, Tennessee. Published by the heirs of Col. Crockett.

plays, and films. Even before his death, a play with a backwoods hero called Nimrod Wildfire had drawn big crowds. Nimrod was modeled after Davy. In 1910 a silent film glamorized Davy's death at the Alamo. In the 1950s, Disney brought him back to life in a popular television series. The great John Wayne played Davy in the 1960 film, *The Alamo*.

"I can't understand [my fame]," Davy wrote, ". . . therefore I put all the facts down, leaving the reader free to take his choice of them."[4]

The real man, he might have added, is best summed up by his motto:

I have this rule for others when I'm dead,
Be always sure you're right—Then Go Ahead! [5]

NOTES BY CHAPTER

Chapter 1

1. Mark Derr, *The Frontiersman: The Real Life and Many Legends of Davy Crockett* (New York: Morrow, 1993), pp. 246–247.

2. James Wakefield Burke, *David Crockett: The Man Behind the Myth* (Austin, Tex.: Eakin Press, 1984), p. 243.

3. Burke, p. 241.

4. Dan Kilgore, *How Did Davy Die?* (College Station, Tex.: Texas A&M University Press, 1978), p. 16.

5. Kilgore, p. 14.

Chapter 2

1. Robert Quackenbush, *Quit Pulling My Leg!: A Story of Davy Crockett* (New York: Prentice-Hall, 1987), p. 10.

2. Mark Derr, *The Frontiersman: The Real Life and Many Legends of Davy Crockett* (New York: Morrow, 1993), pp. 47–48.

3. Davy Crockett, *The Adventures of Davy Crockett: Told Mostly by Himself* (New York: Charles Scribner's Sons, 1934), pp. 32–33.

4. Stewart H. Holbrook, *Davy Crockett* (New York: Random House, 1955), p. 37.

Chapter 3

1. Howard Zinn, *A People's History of the United States* (New York: Harper Colophon Books, 1980), p. 126.

2. Davy Crockett, *The Adventures of Davy Crockett, Told Mostly by Himself* (New York: Scribner, 1934), pp. 53–54.

3. Mark Derr, *The Frontiersman: The Real Life and Many Legends of Davy Crockett* (New York: Morrow, 1993), pp. 67–68.

4. James Wakefield Burke, *David Crockett: The Man Behind the Myth* (Austin, Tex.: Eakin Press, 1984), p. 76.

5. Derr, p. 71.

6. Crockett, p. 75.

7. Ibid., p. 76.

8. Derr, p. 78.

Chapter 4

1. Robert Quackenbush, *Quit Pulling My Leg!: A Story of Davy Crockett* (New York: Prentice-Hall, 1987), p. 20.

2. Mark Derr, *The Frontiersman: The Real Life and Many Legends of Davy Crockett* (New York: Morrow, 1993), p. 80.

3. Davy Crockett, *The Adventures of Davy Crockett: Told Mostly by Himself* (New York: Scribner, 1934), p. 99.

4. Derr, pp. 88–89.

5. James A. Shackford, *David Crockett: The Man and the Legend* (Chapel Hill, N.C.: University of North Carolina Press, 1956), p. 39.

Chapter 5

1. *The Life of Davy Crockett, the Original Humorist and Irrepressible Backwoodsman* (New York: Burt, 1902), p. 106.

2. James A. Shackford, *David Crockett: The Man and the Legend* (Chapel Hill, N.C.: University of North Carolina Press, 1956), p. 50.

3. Mark Derr, *The Frontiersman: The Real Life and Many Legends of Davy Crockett* (New York: Morrow, 1993), p. 102.

4. Shackford, p. 64.

5. *The Life of Davy Crockett*, pp. 128–129.

6. Derr, p. 128.

Chapter 6

1. *The Life of Davy Crockett, the Original Humorist and Irrepressible Backwoodsman* (New York: Burt, 1902), p. 131.

2. Mark Derr, *The Frontiersman: The Real Life and Many Legends of Davy Crockett* (New York: Morrow, 1993), pp. 131–132.

3. Stewart H. Holbrook, *Davy Crockett* (New York: Random House, 1955), p. 103.

4. Davy Crockett, *The Adventures of Davy Crockett, Told Mostly By Himself* (New York: Scribner's, 1934), p. 128.

5. Holbrook, p. 116.

6. Derr, pp. 139–140.

Chapter 7

1. Robert Quackenbush, *Quit Pulling My Leg!: A Story of Davy Crockett* (New York: Prentice-Hall, 1987), p. 29.

2. Mark Derr, *The Frontiersman: The Real Life and Many Legends of Davy Crockett* (New York: Morrow, 1993), p. 145.

3. Quoted in Derr, pp. 150–151.

Chapter 8

1. James A. Shackford, *Davy Crockett: The Man and the Legend* (Chapel Hill, N.C.: University of North Carolina Press, 1956), p. 127.

2. J. M. Keating, *History of Memphis and Shelby County, Tennessee,* vol. I (New York: Mason, 1888), p. 176ff.

3. Tom Townsend, *Davy Crockett: An American Hero* (Austin, Tex.: Eakin Press, 1987), p. 47.

4. Mark Derr, *The Frontiersman: The Real Life and Many Legends of Davy Crockett* (New York: Morrow, 1993), p. 169.

5. Constance Rourke, *Davy Crockett* (New York: Harcourt Brace Jovanovich, 1962), p. 135.

6. Derr, p. 184.

7. Shackford, p. 143.

8. Townsend, p. 48.

Chapter 9

1. Tom Townsend, *Davy Crockett: An American Hero* (Austin, Tex.: Eakin Press, 1987), p. 53.

2. James Wakefield Burke, *David Crockett: The Man Behind the Myth* (Austin, Tex.: Eakin Press, 1984), p. 194.

3. *The Life of Davy Crockett, the Original Humorist and Irrepressible Backwoodsman* (New York: Burt, 1902), p. 253.

4. Ibid., p. ix.

5. Mark Derr, *The Frontiersman: The Real Life and Many Legends of Davy Crockett* (New York: Morrow, 1993), p. 202.

GLOSSARY

Alamo—A former mission in San Antonio that was fortified by rebellious Texans in 1836.

almanac—A yearly publication that contains charts, tables, and lists of useful data.

amendment—A change or addition to a proposed law.

bayonet—A long, sharp knife attached to the muzzle end of a rifle.

bleeding—An outmoded medical technique that treated illness by draining blood from a patient's veins. Bleeding was used widely in the 1800s, but did more harm than good.

bounty—A payment made to hunters who kill animals that prey on domestic livestock.

distillery—A plant where whiskey or other liquors are made from fruits and grains.

dowry—Money or property a bride brings to her husband as part of the marriage contract.

fandango—Spanish for a party with lively dancing.

flatboat—A raft-like boat with a cabin on the deck. Flatboats, which were built of heavy logs, carried cargo downstream. They could not be sailed upstream.

gristmill—A building equipped with large millstones for grinding grain into flour or meal.

justice of the peace—Official who presides over the lowest level of county courts.

legislature—A lawmaking body elected by the voters of a state or nation.

malaria—A disease transmitted by the bite of a female *anopheles* mosquito.

militia—Part-time soldiers who are called to duty in times of emergency.

mission—A group of buildings established by missionaries as the base for their efforts to bring religion and education to native peoples.

musket—A smoothbore, muzzle-loading shoulder gun.

patent medicine—A medicine that can be purchased without a prescription. In the 1800s, patent medicines were widely used, even though most had little medical value.

pensions—Monthly payments made to ex-soldiers and other retired workers.

precedent—An act or decision that is used as a guide for future decisions.

scouts—Skilled woodsmen who guide their own troops and keep watch on enemy forces.

session—The official period during which a legislature meets and conducts business.

speculator—Someone who engages in risky ventures in hopes of making a quick profit.

still—A covered kettle in which vapor from a boiling liquid is collected. If the liquid is a fermented mash, the vapor condenses as whiskey.

tariff—A tax on goods imported into a country.

teamster—The driver of a team of horses or oxen.

MORE GOOD READING ABOUT
DAVY CROCKETT

Arpad, Joseph, ed. *A Narrative of the Life of David Crockett of the State of Tennessee, Written by Himself.* New Haven, Conn.: College and University Press, 1972.

Burke, James Wakefield. *David Crockett: The Man Behind the Myth.* Austin, Tex.: Eakin Press, 1984.

Derr, Mark. *The Frontiersman: The Real Life and the Many Legends of Davy Crockett.* New York: Morrow, 1993.

Holbrook, Stewart. *Davy Crockett.* New York: Random House, 1955.

Quackenbush, Robert. *Quit Pulling My Leg!: A Story of Davy Crockett.* New York: Prentice-Hall, 1987.

Rourke, Constance. *Davy Crockett.* New York: Harcourt Brace Jovanovich, 1962.

Shackford, James Atkins. *David Crockett: The Man and the Legend.* Chapel Hill, N.C.: University of North Carolina Press, 1956.

Townsend, Tom. *Davy Crockett: An American Hero.* Austin, Tex.: Eakin Press, 1987.

INDEX